Teddy's Christmas Cards

side A

Place side A
on top of
side B
like this.

Front view

Turn them over.
Fold tabs from A
and glue to back of B.

Back view

side A

Merry
Christmas

Merry
Christmas

side B

Cut out
along
black lines.

Match each numbered
tab to the numbers on
the mobile tree.

Teddy's Mobile Pieces

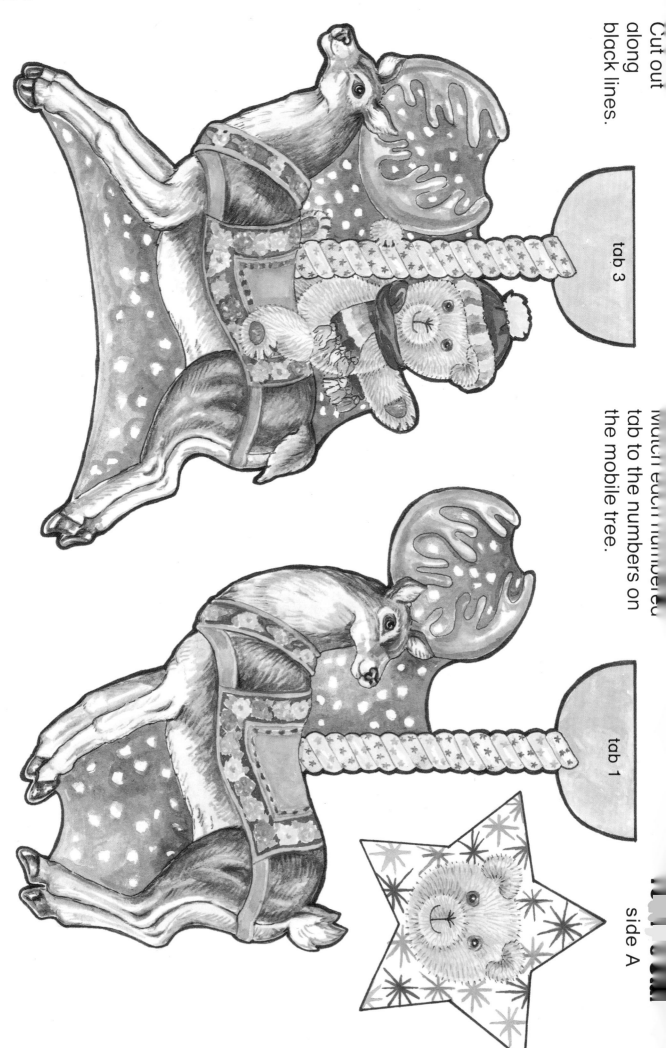

tab 3

tab 1

side A

Tab **A** Glue this side.

3

4

7

8

Sheet 4

24

11

7

Merry Christmas

13

12

23

19

20

1

8

21

Sheet 5

Teddy's Countdown Stickers

1 Teddy goes shopping.

2 What will he buy?

3 Teddy chooses some Christmas cards.

4 Teddy will need plenty of food.

5 He is going to make a big Christmas dinner.

6 What a lot of packages he has!

7 Teddy wraps his gift

8 Then he mails some cards to his friends.

9 What is Teddy going to buy now?

10 He has bought a Christmas tree!

11 Teddy finds last year's decorations in the attic.

12 It's fun decorating the tree.

13 Teddy's neighbors have finished their tree.

14 Look at all these presents waiting for Christmas Day!

15 Stockings are hanging up.

16 Party balloons.

17 What has he been given for Christmas?

18 Here is a Nativity scene.

19 The mailman has delivered lots of cards for Teddy.

20 Teddy goes caroling.

21 There is plenty of snow to make a snowman.

22 Teddy has fun on his sled.

23 Teddy's Christmas dinner is ready.

24 Are you ready? Here comes Santa Claus!

Merry Christmas, Teddy!

Teddy's Countdown to Christmas

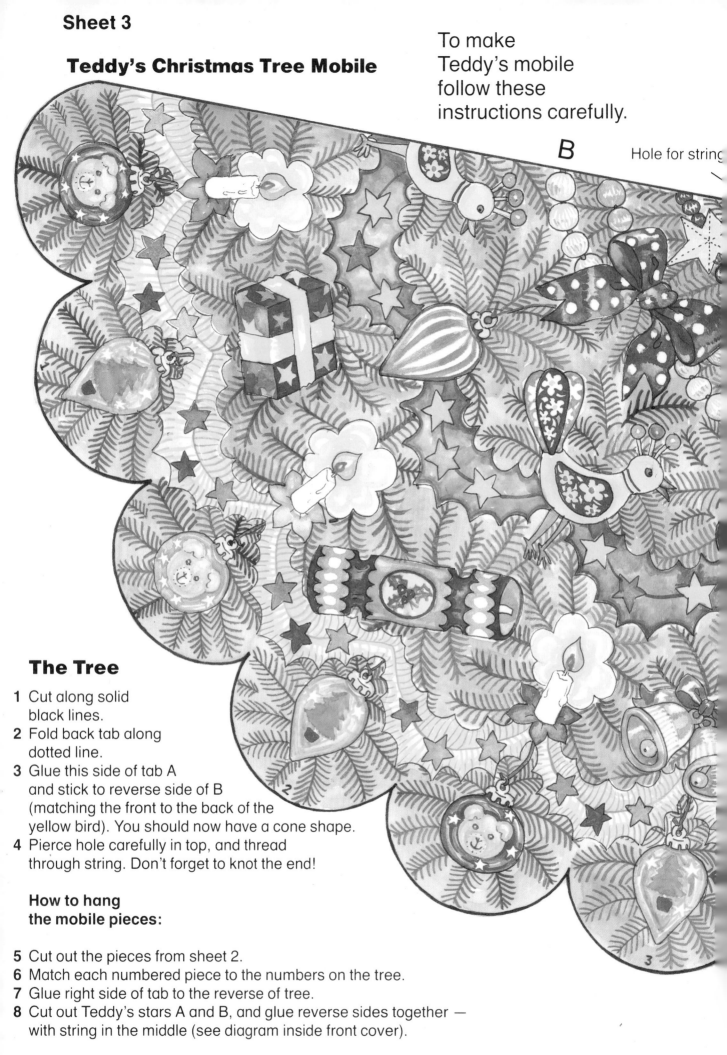

Sheet 3

Teddy's Christmas Tree Mobile

To make Teddy's mobile follow these instructions carefully.

B

Hole for string

The Tree

1 Cut along solid black lines.
2 Fold back tab along dotted line.
3 Glue this side of tab A and stick to reverse side of B (matching the front to the back of the yellow bird). You should now have a cone shape.
4 Pierce hole carefully in top, and thread through string. Don't forget to knot the end!

How to hang the mobile pieces:

5 Cut out the pieces from sheet 2.
6 Match each numbered piece to the numbers on the tree.
7 Glue right side of tab to the reverse of tree.
8 Cut out Teddy's stars A and B, and glue reverse sides together — with string in the middle (see diagram inside front cover).

Teddy's mobile is now ready to hang.

tab 2

tab 6

tab 4

tab 5

Full instructions on sheet 3

Teddy's Star
side B